G000123663

There was once a boatyard at Perelle called La Tablette, which was between a cottage of that name and the Perelle boat-launching slip. It looked like this in 1925, before the ramshackle building made of rough tarred planks was pulled down. This clapboard building, attached to a cottage now known as La Colline, was the home of John Savident and his wife Lydia. It was here that all the Perelle fishing boats were hauled up for winter on land owned by John Paint. Each boat-owner's place was staked out with stones. The area was strewn with old willow crabpots, store boxes for shellfish, oars, flat-bottomed boats and all the paraphenalia which added to the chaotic charm of such places. Among the boats kept in this yard until after the last war were: *Mermaid* (W. Jehan); *Esperance* (Wm,. Jehan); *Watch* (Alfred Brehant); *Two Brothers* (Wm., Queripel); *Alice* (Alfred Savident). Author's drawing from a photograph taken by the late Charles H. Toms in 1925.

Guernsey's Forgotten Past

A section of one of a number of beautiful cast iron gates which adorn the Lower Vegetable Market, St Peter Port, which was completed in 1879 to designs by Francis Chambers.

Guernsey's Forgotten Past

Carel Toms

Phillimore

1992

Published by
PHILLIMORE & CO. LTD.,
Shopwyke Hall, Chichester, Sussex

© Carel Toms, 1992

ISBN 0 85033 850 6

Printed and bound in Great Britain by
BIDDLES LTD.,
Guildford, Surrey

List of Illustrations

Frontispiece: Gates, Lower Vegetable Market, St Peter Port.

Acknowledgements

The author is grateful to the following for the help they have given and the interest they have shown in assisting in the compilation of this book: D. F. Ashplant, Peter Brehaut, Eric Clark, Doris Cook, Don Le Couteur, Brian Dyke, the editor of the *Journal* of the Guernsey Society, Peter Falla, Marie de Garis, the late Wilson Gaudion, John Girard, the Guille-Allès Library, A. O. Hamon, Mervyn Harwood, Ken Hill, Peter Kinnersly, La Société Guernesiaise, Dick Leaman, L. James Marr, Edwin Martel, John McCormack, H. Nicolle, T. F. Priaulx, the Priaulx Library, Lloyd Robilliard, Ray Russel, the late Eric W. Sharp, States of Guernsey Customs and Excise, the late Charles H. Toms, George Torode, and many others. Other photographs and drawings are either by the author or from his collection.

Foreword

Guernsey's Forgotten Past is a book which has strayed from the pattern of five previous volumes of old photographs of the Bailiwick. It includes chapters on local subjects never before investigated, such as our magnificent Victorian carved doors, our men of the fishing industry and a detailed look at the island's wells and dated pumps.

Four earlier volumes were the joint work of Victor Coysh and the present author. The fifth was undertaken by myself and this present volume of photographs and drawings dips further into the island's fascinating past.

It touches on people, events and places and a host of other aspects of life in the Bailiwick which has totally vanished. The pictures are set out in sections and have come into my hands from official sources as well as a great number of readers far and wide.

Without their help and especially the encouragement and advice of Victor Coysh, who read the manuscript and offered valuable ideas and suggestions, this volume would never have been compiled.

CAREL TOMS

Carved Front Doors

Throughout the Victorian period a number of island cabinet-makers, notably Richard Guille (1808-95), John Burgess (1814-1904), Nicholas Robilliard (1817-98) and Henry Marquand (*c.*1890s), made carvings for exterior house doors which are unique to Guernsey. Little is known about these men or their contemporaries but their designs and craftsmanship are to be seen in every one of the island's ten parishes.

When these doors were being installed it was during a period of burgeoning prosperity and many people had money to spend. Quarrying granite, growing and exporting grapes and flowers were in full swing and this was followed by the first export of maincrop tomatoes in 1884.

The wealthier horticulturists were building substantial villas with decoration – interior and exterior – to match their considerable means. Communications by sea to the markets of the United Kingdom had vastly improved and island builders were not slow to follow British trends, adding their own quirky additions. Exterior decoration manifested itself from rooftops to cast-iron railings. Fancy chimney pots, crested ridge-tiles, crockets, dentils, plaster work, fretwork bargeboards in wood and cast-iron vied with doorcases surrounded with heavily decorated console brackets.

One manifestation of the affluence of the period is the number of front doors which bear the work of skilled carvers. How this fashion started or by whom is not known but it does appear to be an additional symbol of wealth which can still be seen on the front doors of more than 90 houses.

All these doors bear the hallmark of individual craftsmen who were working solely to please a customer. In another age, it has been suggested, a knock on such a highly ornamented door and one might expect to be greeted by a maid holding a silver salver upon which you would deposit your card.

At the last count the number of carved doors in each parish was as follows; St Peter Port, 35; Vale, 22; St Sampson's, 14; Castel, 7; St Martin's, 6; St Pierre du Bois, 5; St Andrew's, 3; Torteval, 2; Forest, 2 and St Saviour's, 1.

It is almost a century or so since the last of these doors was made and there is no doubt there were many more than are to be seen today. Only in recent years have islanders become more conscious of the heritage left by the Victorians. Whilst many doors have been ruthlessly destroyed and have been replaced with off-the-shelf glass-panelled doors in order to shed more light into otherwise dark hallways, those which are left are now looked upon as precious heirlooms and preservation orders have been placed on the majority by the States of Guernsey Ancient Monuments Committee.

Among the many cabinet-makers known to have worked in Guernsey, four names have been identified as having made carvings for doors. However, only one is positively known as having made a particular pair of doors. He was Richard Guille, a furniture-maker, who had a workshop at Emma Place, Pedvin Street, where he inserted a pair of carved doors at nos. 1 and 2. The second one has, unfortunately, been completely defaced. Guille named the property after his daughter. He is also known to have made wardrobes, picture frames and sideboards.

Nicholas Robilliard was another cabinet-maker. He had a workshop adjacent to Shrubwood, St Jacques, the family home in St Peter Port. One of his doors is known to have been installed at what is now *Lilyvale Hotel*, Hougue du Pommier, Castel. Unfortunately the door was lost during modernisation.

John Burgess appears in a list of cabinet-makers in the *Guernsey Almanack* of 1861, and is thought to have had a workshop at Glategny Esplanade and later in Victoria Road. In the 1899 *Kelly's Directory* of the Channel Islands, Burgess Brothers of Lower St James' Street are listed as being cabinet-makers. Burgess is thought to have carved the splendid door at La Pompe, La Contrée des Mouilpieds, St Martin's.

Henry Marquand had a workshop at 26 Le Bordage, St Peter Port and was a renowned cabinet-maker and carver. Not only did he make 'door ornaments' but he also carved butter marks. An Ordinance laid down that when butter was prepared for sale in a pat, it had to conform to a round shape, 'bearing on one of its plane surfaces an imprint consisting of a design surrounded by the name and address of the producer in a circular outline'. This applied only to Guernsey, Herm and Jethou. Each stamp was carved in reverse and gave a clear impression of the farmer's name and address. There were half-pound as well as one-pound 'forms' and most were of a highly artistic nature. When the States took over the total distribution of milk and set up the States Dairy in 1951, the practice of making butter on the farms ceased and the carved 'forms' were no longer used.

In 1866 there were at least 14 cabinet-makers in Guernsey and it is highly likely that more than those listed above were also engaged in making door ornamentation in wood.

There are two carved doors which are outstandingly different to those elsewhere in the island. One is the double door at Le Vallon, St Martin's. The other is at La Jaonière (formerly Mayfield) at Route de la Croix au Bailif, St Andrew's.

When Isaac Carey (1758-1828) purchased Le Vallon in 1804, it was no more than a large farmhouse. He altered it considerably to accommodate his 14 children. Isaac died in 1828 and De Vic Carey (1789-1876), the fourth son, set about enlarging it. The character of the house was in a state of metamorphosis for years and its style changed from Georgian to Victorian Gothick.

De Vic Carey owned a successful wine business, importing wine from Spain. He was arguably the most successful owner of privateers in the island and became a very rich man. He spent a great deal of time in Spain and brought back architectural sketches which he passed on to his builder to interpret. The pair of doors at Le Vallon depict two splendid palm trees standing in relief and have a distinct North African flavour. The historian T. F. Priaulx believes they were the work of Burgess. The palms are deeply carved, with the background in light relief. The door knob is also carved.

These doors have been partially examined in recent years when the owner discovered rot in the lower part of one door. A two-foot section was removed and replaced by cabinet-maker S. Waterman. He found the door had been made up in layers, to which the carved surface sections had been glued.

Vale

1. Bordeaux House, at Les Grippios, Vale, was probably built between 1843 and 1857. It was inherited by Jean Brache who sold it to Nicolas Etienne Martin and his wife (née Brache). The lead-fronted pump box adjacent to the house bears the date 1873 and the inscription 'N. Martin, M. Brache'. Mr. Martin died in 1909. His wife died six years later and the property passed to her nephew, Stephen Martin Le Conte. It remained in the Le Conte family until the death of Stephen Le Conte in 1976. This photograph of the house is thought to date from *c.*1915 and shows from left to right: Pierre Mahy Le Conte, Stephen Le Conte, Mrs. Mary Martin and Mrs. Julia Le Conte. In 1977 the house was sold out of the family.

2. The very fine carved door at Bordeaux House shows bunches of grapes, flowers and foliage. Originally it was protected inside the beautiful glass porch. It is now on the east gable which borders Les Grippios Lane.

3. This heavy carving of bunches of grapes occurs on a house which is part of The Laurels, in the Vale Avenue, Vale.

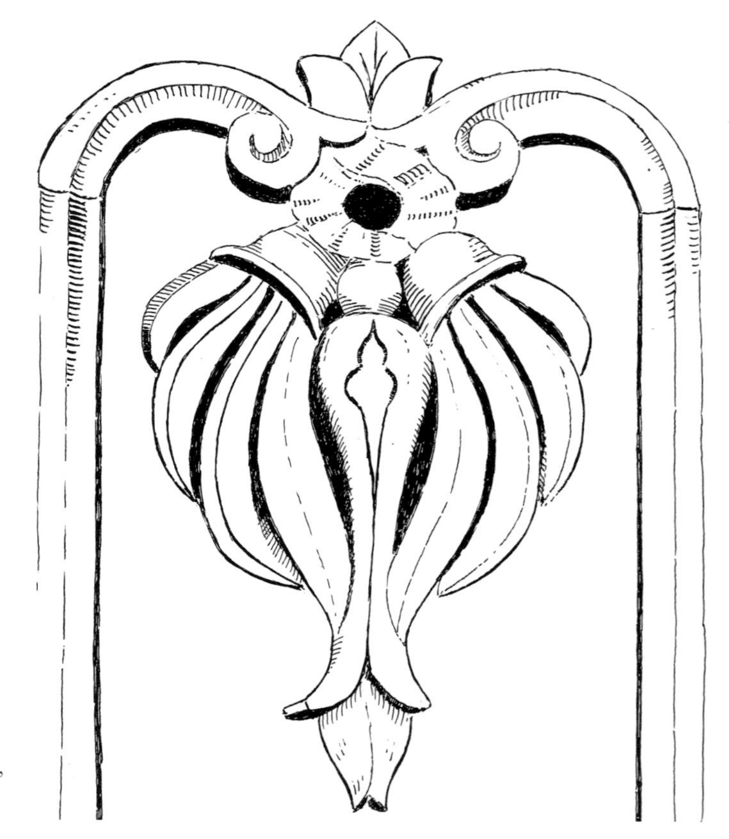

4. The decorated door at Les Hautgards, Noirmont, Pleinheaume, Vale, has a sub-tropical look with carvings of what could be bananas.

St Martin's

5. The magnificent double door at Le Vallon, St Martin's, with its pair of palms, has a distinct North African look.

6. A close-up of the left side of the door at Le Vallon, St Martin's, shows the intricacy of the carving.

7. This carved door at La Pompe, Le Contrée des Mouilpieds, St Martin's is attributed to Burgess and must have replaced an earlier door. The house bears two dates on the arch: 'TTLT 1606' and '1863 JMDMG'. The latter date is probably when the door was inserted.

8. La Quinta at La Rue Maze, St Martin's, is now an hotel and has retained its antique door carving.

St Sampson's

10. The door at Meadow Villa, Route de Vaugrat, St Sampson's, has an intricate floral design picked out in green, black, yellow and red. The carving within the panel is mounted separately and can be unscrewed for repainting.

12. The carving on the door at the private hotel *Antigua*, Les Grandes Maisons Road, St Sampson's. The house is said to have been owned by a ship's captain who often sailed to the West Indies.

9. For sheer exotic decoration, this beautifully carved fruit and flower motif shows an apple, pear, plum and a bunch of grapes set off against a leafy background. It is all picked out in colour and is on the front door of the Victorian house, Glenview, Les Effards Road, St Sampson's.

11. The door at Gypsland, Les Grandes Maisons Road, St Sampson's, bears a unique floral motif.

St Andrew's

13. Of all the island's carved doors, this one at La Jaonière (formerly Mayfield) at Route de la Croix au Bailif, St Andrew's, is perhaps the finest. It represents a tree with full foliage and flowers, possibly daffodils, at its base. The initials 'H and JSN' and the date 1875 incised over the arch indicate when the house may have been completed and the door inserted.

14. Knapp House, at the Rohais de Haut, St Andrew's, is owned by the States of Guernsey. Its well-built porch not only bears a carved door but has one of only two red-granite doorsteps so far discovered carved with scrolls and a Guernsey crest. The other is at a house in Allez Street, St Peter Port.

St Peter Port

15. *(Above left)* Another intricate carving incorporating flowers is at no. 1 Escallonia, Mount Durand, St Peter Port.

16. *(Above)* This complicated carving of leaves and flowers is on the door at no. 1 Newlands, Mount Durand, St Peter Port.

17. *(Left)* One of a pair of doors of Emma Place, Pedvin Street, St Peter Port, once the home and workshop of Richard Guille, the carver. This pattern occurs with variations in other parishes.

18. The carving on this door at *Norfolk Lodge Hotel*, Doyle Road, St Peter Port, is quite a simple flourish of leaves within two panels, one of which is studded.

Torteval

19. The beautifully maintained carved door at Le Petit Manoir (formerly Le Haut) on La Route de Pleinmont in Torteval parish is on the front of an 18th-century house which was thoroughly 'Victorianised' during the 19th century when the door was probably inserted. It is complete in every detail, the two carved sections being neatly married together within a panel.

20. One other surviving door in Torteval parish is at La Viltone, Rue de la Lague. It is very similar to that at Le Petit Manoir and may have come from the same workshop.

St Saviours and Forest

21. This door of unknown provenance was found on a rubbish dump in the 1970s and brought to the author's attention. It lay in a shed for several years and in 1990 was finally installed as the back door to Richmond Cottage, St Saviour's. It is the only one of its kind in the parish.

22. This door once adorned La Roberge, the erstwhile home of Denys Corbet, primitive painter of farm animals, at La Roberge Lane, Forest, until 1989 when it was removed and replaced with a modern door. There was no other like it in the island; a single carving with tear drop leaves and an ornamental horseshoe, with panelling decorations to match. The parish now has one house left with a carved front door, at Le Bourg de Haut.

Butter Forms

23a & b. When Guernsey had several hundred small farms where butter was made, an Ordinance laid down that when it was prepared for sale in a pat, it had to conform to a round shape 'bearing on one of its plane surfaces an imprint consisting of a design surrounded by the name and address of the producer in a circular outline, and shall include any portion of such circular pat as such'. The Ordinance applied only to Guernsey, Herm and Jethou. It was forbidden to sell imported butter in the 'Guernsey Form'. Each stamp was carved in reverse and gave a clear impression of the farmer's name and address. There were half-pound as well as one-pound 'forms' and most were of a highly artistic nature. When retailed in the market, pats were originally placed on cabbage leaves until the invention of greaseproof paper. When the States took over the total distribution of milk and set up the States Dairy in 1951, the practice of making butter for public sale ceased. Two farms at Les Grand Moulins (King's Mills) Castel were run by the de Garis family. Ernest de Garis farmed at Myrtle Place (now *Hotel Fleur du Jardin*) and his son, Ernest John, farmed at St Leddard's, not far away. In those days few farmers kept more than seven or eight cows. These carved wooden 'forms' are four-and-a-half inches in diameter and were for making half-pound pats. One-pound pats were moulded on five-and-a-half inch 'forms'.

The Mackerel Drifters

Apart from a brief comeback in 1961, drift netting for mackerel off Guernsey effectively ended in the early 1930s. Mackerel fishing started in the 1870s when big shoals were being caught in nets as the drifters moved up the English Channel. Cornish fishermen were exploiting both pilchards and mackerel, and Guernsey entrepreneurs and fishermen were not slow to see the commercial possibilities.

They were quick, it appears, to copy what the Cornishmen were doing, going so far as to buy second-hand Cornish boats and nets for use off Guernsey, believing, perhaps, that these boats would do better than those built in the island to do the same work. The boat owners were not necessarily fishermen themselves. Often they provided the capital to invest in a boat and employed a skipper who would recruit a crew of five or six other fishermen.

The building of boats for this fishery was an industry in itself. The majority were built in the island in various boatyards; but they also came from Sark, Jersey and Cornwall. There may at one time have been as many as 24 drifters working out of the small havens of Rocquaine, Perelle and Vazon on the west coast. These boats varied greatly in length and tonnage. Drifters were usually fully decked. There were also several different rigs in use until the 1920s, when petrol engines started to be widely used and there was a decline in the total reliance on sail. The boats fished for some 12 weeks, from May until August, when they were laid up at St Sampson's harbour.

It is unclear who was the first to start the fishery but it is generally considered to have been the Le Couteurs of Rocquaine. The Guernsey branch of the family came from Jersey in the 1830s to start a business as wholesale merchants at Le Gron, St Saviour's. In 1840, the house known as Alderbaran, at the foot of Le Coudré hill, was purchased and run also as an hotel, known as *Rocquaine Commercial Hotel.* The Le Couteurs became suppliers of nets and gear for fishing boats, including pitch, tar and cutch for tanning nets. The hotel catered for picnic parties and tourists and also branched out into other fields.

For mackerel drifting, the Cornishmen preferred the rig known as the dipping lug, whilst the Guernsey fishermen preferred the schooner rig, the cutter or the yawl. None of these boats had any power other than that provided by the wind or the strength of the crew, when they had to row in calm weather.

24. The drifter *Rosalind* (GU 140) was owned by Elie Robilliard of Roseneath, Torteval and was cutter rigged. It is likely that this 35½ ft. eight-tonner came originally from Cornwall. She was first registered in Guernsey in the name of John W. Savident of Perelle, in May 1906. She went to Elie Robilliard in 1911 and ended her days in 1927. She had two known skippers: A. de la Mare and Tom de Carteret. Photograph by Peter Brehaut.

25. What remained of this house after the Germans had removed the gable was demolished in 1991. In the days of the mackerel fishery it was known as The Casquets (after the famous lighthouse). It was the home of Emile Ashplant, whose son, Henry, was 86 in 1991 and remembers when drifters were heading for their moorings in darkness. The crews watched for a lighted oil lamp in the gable window to guide them in.

26. Henry Ashplant was born in 1905, went out fishing in boats at a very early age and at 14 worked in the 36 ft. mackerel drifter *Joli* (GU 37), which was built in 1856 at St Sampson's and owned by John Martin, who kept her at Vazon. For a short spell Henry went to sea and was shipwrecked. He returned to Guernsey and in 1924 bought the cutter *Wonder* (GU 132), built in 1896. (*See* Men of the Sea.)

27. When preparing to go to sea, the mackerel drifters kept at Le Crocq du Sud were loaded with 30 fathom lengths of net on the beach. The boats would leave here at dusk and return at dawn. The net mesh size was quite critical and on moonlit nights or when the water became phosphorescent fewer fish were caught. Guernsey artist Peter Le Lievre painted this watercolour in the 1870s.

28a. When fishing was at its height, these cottages at Les Issues, Rocquaine, were the homes of fishermen and the crews of the mackerel drifters. Tom de Carteret, or 'Le p'tit Tom' as he was known, lived here and was a one-time skipper of the drifter *Rosalind*.

28b. Tom de Carteret is remembered as a character with a very wrinkled face who chewed tobacco and liked his drink. It was said that although he could neither read nor write, all he had to do to find his way in foggy weather was merely to dangle a hand in the water to determine the current.

29. Edmund de la Mare, skipper of the *Souvenir* (GU 101) in 1928. He is shown making crabpots in Le Couteur's yard in 1935. *Souvenir* arrived in the island in 1918 and was finally broken up in 1940.

30. At Alderbaran, where the Le Couteurs operated from the large building and yard, nets and gear were stored at the foot of Le Coudré, known as La Halle. In the nearby Bark House the nets were tanned in cutch, an extract of Indian plants rich in tannin. It was boiled in this large copper and young oak bark in powder form was added when it was available. The nets were left to steep in the mixture for at least two days and nights. The tanning liquor mixed with coal tar was found to preserve nets much longer.

31. Among the fleet of drifters was the 40 ft. cutter rigged *Marie Louise* (GU 27). She was owned by George Henry Tucker of La Fontenelle Farm, St Saviour's. His granddaughter, Mrs. J. E. Martel, possesses this fine photograph of the *Marie Louise* racing under reduced canvas at the 1913 Rocquaine Regatta. She was usually moored at Perelle, where her skipper was John Savident.

32a. During misty weather or thick fog, a horn – *le Corne à breune* – was blown at intervals by fishermen. Traditionally this was a tropical conch shell. They were brought home by sailors from the West Indies and elsewhere. Every fisherman kept one in his boat, either to sound off in fog or to draw the attention of passing craft.

32b. These primitive trumpets, with the apex filed away to provide a mouthpiece, could be heard for a considerable distance. They were also used by quarry foremen to warn workers of impending blasting and by farmers to call in their men. Blowing a horn in this picture is a modern fisherman, Edwin Martel.

33. There was a brief comeback of mackerel drifting off Guernsey in 1961 when exactly the same methods were used as in the old days. This was organised by Ken Quentin, owner of the 45 ft. *Dieu te Garde*, whose skipper was Art Hamon. The cotton nets used came from St Ives, Cornwall. The exercise was only partly successful as about this time 'feathering' for mackerel had started in earnest and the drift net project was dropped. The *Dieu te Garde* is seen here at the Albert Dock being loaded with nets.

People and Events

34. A charabanc outing of a group of English quarry managers who were holding a conference in the island, *c.* 1925. The bus is stopped outside the offices of John Mowlem's on the North Side.

35. The stone-cracking yards at L'Ongrée, Les Monmains, North Side in about 1898. Houses at the Maresquet can be seen in the distance. The site is now used by Ernest J. Henry Ltd. Boys as young as nine worked in the yards after school.

36. The Hougue Noirmont stone quarry, now a sea farm, was one of the last to be worked. It was owned by the Falla family and Peter Falla is seen standing in front of the crane which lifted stone from the quarry floor. This photograph was taken *c.*1948.

37. It took nine horses to transport the stone upon which Victor Hugo's statue stands in Candie Gardens from Crève Coeur, Clos du Valle, where it had been part of an outcrop near the beach. The quarry foreman at the time was N. Pinchemain and among the drivers were D. Bisset and D. Renouf. The enormous stone was photographed as the horse-drawn cart was passing what is now the Marine and General Engineers Ltd. Shipyard on the North Side. It is hard to imagine how this old 'low loader' negotiated St Julian's Avenue and Candie Road into the grounds. The statue was unveiled in July 1914.

38. Peter Grisel was probably the last maker of granite setts for export to the United Kingdom. They were shaped into three basic sizes: four inches by five inches; three inches by seven inches; and in four-inch cubes, known locally as 'gumbals'.

39. A. and F. Manuelle's stone-cracking yards, crushing plant and windmill at Longue Hougue, South Side, St Sampson's, *c.*1900. Delancey monument can be seen in the distance. The water-filled quarry now comprises part of the island's water supply.

40. Morley Russell was a renowned tinsmith, whose tiny workshop was near Jerbourg, St Martin's. He became famous, along with his two sons, Arthur and Fred, for making Guernsey milk cans, whose practical use was eclipsed when milk ceased to be retailed from door to door by individual farmers and was delivered in churns to a centralised dairy. The can-making tradition still continues, however, and cans – often made in silver – are frequently given as parting gifts to visiting dignitaries.

41. A brass bachin being used to make jam by Jim Martin in 1950. He lived at La Mare, St Martin's.

42. Thomas Bichard, on the far right of the picture, was a Guernsey seaman who served in many local vessels, both sail and steam, from 1876 until 1920. In this photograph he is on board a local trading vessel. He also served in the brigs *Reaper*, *Prince Alfred* and *The Sisters*. After working in coastal traders, he served in the local steamers *Rescue*, *Assistance* and *Helper*. Mr. Bichard was the father of Thomas Bichard who ran the well-known grocery shop in Les Canichers between the 1920s and the 1950s. The picture was taken at Creux Harbour, Sark.

43. On 6 March 1938 the 228-tonne *S.S. Tommeliten* was bound for Guernsey from Port Talbot with a cargo of anthracite coal. In dense fog she struck a rock off Bordeaux Harbour and finished up beached with a three-foot diameter gaping hole in her bows. She was refloated the same evening and limped into St Sampson's harbour.

44. President of the Guernsey Sea Anglers' Club, Gervase F. Peek, on board his boat *Nancy* with four of the 13 competitors who used five different boats for an angling contest in Bellegrève Bay in June 1938.

45. The music for functions at the *Hotel Beaulieu*, St Martin's in 1938, was provided by Dixie Dene and his band.

46. The Palace Theatre, otherwise known as Billy Bartlett's, in St Julian's Avenue, was a favourite venue for such events as roller-skating carnivals. This one took place in February 1938.

47. St Sampson's Methodist Schoolroom was the venue for this party for the children of employees of Leale Ltd., in January 1936.

MARION BOWDITCH
STAN
BOBBY.

48. Miss Muriel Luckie and her Guernsey Junior Choir which achieved notable success at the Jersey Eisteddfod in 1935, winning the Donaldson shield. *Left to right from back row:* D. Luckie, F. Bowditch, G. Le Page, B. Mollett, R. Priaulx, Y. Le Goff, D. Jones, G. Bent, G. Lowe, I. Robinson, N. Le Noury, N. Squire, M. Wyatt, B. Renouf, J. Paul, G. Torode, V. Hammond, S. Brouard, D. Powditch; D. Barker, M. Duquemin, G. Paul, N. Jones, Miss Luckie, E. Zabiela, B. Sheppard, B. Cook, J. Hamblin, G.Gregg.

49. Two German guns, captured during the First World War, once stood in Victoria Tower Gardens. In January 1938 it was decided to cut them up into pieces and export them for scrap.

50. Messrs. S. M. and T. A. Marquand entered this model farm at the North Show and Battle of Flowers in 1937. It came in second in the motor lorry class. The 'cow' was attended by Sheila and Tommy Marquand.

51. The Island Police Force in 1936. Seated in the centre is Inspector W. R. Schulper. The police sergeants are, *(from left to right):* A. Howlett, C. Le Lievre, J. Langmead, E. Pill, A. J. Langmead, F. Duquemin and F. Banneville. The picture was taken by J. A. Hamson.

52. Christmas Day at the Town hospital in 1935, when 56 men and 34 women sat down to their meal in the day room upstairs. *From left to right:* Deputy Marie Randall, Mrs. H. Norris (assistant matron), F. H. de la Rue (carving), Mr. H. Norris (assistant master), Mrs. S. J. Davidson and her husband (master and matron), John Davidson (their son), Mr. Cecil Stonelake (carving) and Miss Winnie Harvey. The hospital was founded in 1741, ceasing to function in 1984, when it was decided to convert it into a police headquarters.

53. The scene at what was once known as the Country hospital, Castel, on Christmas Day 1935. Standing in front of the Christmas tree about to distribute gifts is Father Christmas (Peter Le Maitre). Also in the group are James Martel, president of the hospital committee *(right)*; the Master and Matron and Sister L. Thorley.

54. One of the many processions to celebrate Guy Fawkes on 5 November 1935 was in the parish of St Saviour's. It set off at Les Raies, where this picture was taken. Those in charge were F. Hegarat, Clifford Le Cras and G. Torode, who led the band.

55. In 1925 the Lieutenant Governor and his wife, Sir Charles and Lady Sackville-West, held their first reception at Saumarez Park. *From left to right:* Sir Edward Ozanne, bailiff, who was knighted in 1921, Baron de Coudenhove, French consul, George Kinnersly; Miqué Kinnersly, Mabel Kinnersly and her husband, Dr. George Kinnersly, who became a jurat of the Royal Court and Lieutenant Bailiff.

56. Miss M. L. Freeman was the teacher at this session at the Domestic Science Centre, Mount Durand in December 1935. This *Evening Press* photograph was taken when the girls present were from the Forest, St Andrew's, St Martin's, St Saviour's, Delancey Catholic, St Sampson's, Hautes Capelles, St Pierre du Bois, Vale and Castel schools. The girls were taught cookery, washing, ironing, baking and metal-polishing.

57. The gunsmith, Walter John Ollivier (1874-1965) was born above a shop which existed at no. 1 Tower Hill, St Peter Port in 1800. It had been started by his great-great grandfather, who, it was said, supplied knives, cutlasses, powder, shot and other items to privateer captains operating from Guernsey. Mr. Ollivier also sharpened saws and other tools. When the grape growing industry was at its height, he would sharpen as many as 3,000 pairs of grape thinning scissors every year.

58. One of the island's last thatchers was William Brouard of Le Catillon, St Pierre du Bois, where he also ran a small farm. He and his wife, who was formerly Ann Esther Martel, were celebrating their diamond wedding when this photograph was taken on 10 May 1930. Mr. Brouard ceased thatching about 1905.

59a. There has been a tea-room at Fermain Bay since 1886. It was first opened in the tower by Mr. and Mrs. W. J. Mallett. Later the business moved to the old powder magazine. When Mrs. Mallett's daughter, Ruby, married Cecil B. Ferguson, they continued the business. In 1929 the Fergusons pioneered a passenger boat service to the bay from St Peter Port. This still continues, the vessel being *Silver Queen* (now *Fermain V*), a veteran of the Dunkirk evacuation. In this picture – taken in the 1920s – Mr. and Mrs. Ferguson are standing in the doorway of the tea-room.

59b. Mrs. W. J. Mallett, wife of the founder of Fermain Bay tea-rooms, sitting on the beach below the tower in 1917 with her daughter – now Mrs. V. Rouilliard.

60. The Methodist Circuit's Bible study class which was conducted by the Rev. J. S. Norman in the Western Parishes in about 1912. *Back row, left to right:* Frank Le Poidevin, John Allez, Wilson Le Lacheur, Ernest Le Page, Ernest Jehan, William Bourgaize, Randolph Robilliard, Edward Brehaut, William Le Lacheur, James Le Page, ? Le Sauvage, John Bourgaize. Front row, left to right: John Le Lacheur, Theo Allez, J. S. Norman, George Langlois, Alfred de la Mare, John de Garis.

61. Officers and teachers of the St Pierrę du Bois Sion Sunday School which celebrated its diamond jubilee in July 1922. Thos. A. Bramley took the photograph.

62. For many years the headquarters of Guppy's mineral water works was at St Clement's Road, St John's. The photograph, which was taken in 1922 shows, *left to right*: W. J. Guppy, J. Duquemin and E. C. Guppy.

63. Machon's of 45 and 47 the Pollet, as the premises looked in about 1905. The business was founded by Alfred Machon (standing with arms akimbo), who as a young man had run away to sea. In 1884 he married Susan Le Poidevin who opene a grocery shop at 26 Cornet Street (now the headquarters of the National Trust of Guernsey). Mr. Machon was a wood worker and started repairing furniture. Later, no. 47 became 'Ye Olde Antique Shoppe' where cabinet-maker James Collivet reigned supreme.

64. The Analytical Tea Company was first established in 1884 by George Spong and occupied premises at 8 Smith Street, now a Guernsey Press Co. Ltd. shop. Mr. Spong moved to 3 Commercial Arcade in 1910 and later the company was owned by Walter John Pontin, who had started to work for Mr. Spong in 1890, when he was sixteen. Mr. Pontin retired about 1948 when the business was sold.

Hundreds of parcels of cigarettes and tobacco were sent from Guernsey to the troops in France during the First World War. With each went a postcard of a leading star of the period 'to liven up a dug out'. The 'Performer' Tobacco Fund was a branch of the Newspapers Patriotic Tobacco Fund. Martins Ltd., of Piccadilly, London, who operated the scheme, was owned by Walter Martin of Guernsey. Parcels were packed at St George's Hall between 1916-18. In charge of the Guernsey end was Frank Fletcher, who later became managing director of the *Royal Hotel* when Walter Martin purchased the premises in 1919. Always a flamboyant character, Martin broke the bank at Monte Carlo in 1920. He died in Guernsey during the German Occupation, aged 75.

65. This picture shows staff of the packing operation on the balcony of St George's Hall.

66a. Before embarking for the Western Front, these members of the Royal Guernsey Light Infantry were encamped at Bourne Park, near Canterbury in 1917. The photograph was taken by Lance Corporal Charles Toms. The soldier in the cap is reading the *Weekly Press*, which in peace as well as in war has carried news from the island to the four corners of the world since 1897.

66b. Guernseymen who went to Canterbury before joining the British Expeditionary Force in France were not forgotten by those at home. This shipment of tomatoes was sent to the troops under canvas at Bourne Park.

67. Breton onion sellers were once a familiar sight, shouting 'Oignons! Oignons!' as they toured the island with their strings of onions across the handlebars of their bicycles.

68. Fred Veale was for some 50 years probably the largest grower and supplier of rhubarb in Guernsey. He built this special greenhouse for the purpose. He even grew rhubarb inside his house. A familiar figure in St Martin's, where he lived, he was often seen cycling to St Peter Port market loaded with rhubarb.

69. Rose Collivet roasting chestnuts at 3 Market Place in the 1860s. She was a fruit and poultry seller and game dealer who also had premises in the Pollet. Oddly, she is wearing Breton style sabots and coiffe in this watercolour.

70. About 1920 the Hon. Marion Saumarez, second daughter of the 4th Lord de Saumarez, took this photograph of a farmer's wife seated on an oxen-shoeing frame at the Forest. The lady remarked to the photographer: 'Pourquoi moi? J'suis pas belle!' The picture appeared in the Guernsey Society's 1963 winter journal. Marion Saumarez was a painter whose work was hung in, among other places, the Paris Salon in 1907.

71. In 1892 the steam tramway between St Peter Port and St Sampson's was replaced by electric. Two years later 'the Petroleur', as it was commonly called, was thought to be the first horseless carriage to arrive in Guernsey. At the controls was Major A. Thom of the Salvation Army. People who had never seen such a monster were said to be frightened as it sped along at 20 miles an hour, racing the trams along Les Banques. This picture was owned by the coal merchant, Ernest J. Henry, who in 1905 was a pioneer driver, owning a De Dion.

72. General Barrington Campbell (later Lord Blythwood) standing on the steps of the Saumarez Park mansion house. He lived there whilst Lieutenant Governor of Guernsey, 1903-8. At the wheel of this very early motor car is Captain Campbell. The chauffeur is standing to the left. Photograph by Aline Head.

73. At Rue du Videcocq, St Pierre du Bois is the ancient farmhouse, La Forge, built between 1400-1550. Adjacent is a *prinseux*, or cider press of about 1848 and stocks for shoeing oxen, the last of their kind to be used in Guernsey. Oxen were employed for ploughing during the Occupation. The farrier was Arthur Dodd, who in November 1956 gave a demonstration to an invited party at the farm which was organised by Advocate W. H. Langlois who had once owned the property. The group saw how cider used to be made from apples partly pulped in a granite crusher and placed in layers in an enormous press.

a. Part of the apple crushing mechanism at La Forge.

b. Arthur Dodd demonstrating how an ox is shod.

John Brehaut was born in Guernsey in 1862. He was the son of George James Brehaut (b.1830) and Rachel Cohu (b.1834). Little is known about his work as an artist on the island but he sketched and drew island scenes of a rural nature in pencil and pen and ink. He lived in England most of his life working for the *Daily Telegraph* and later for the council at Wood Green. He retired to Brightlingsea and died there in 1958, aged ninety-six.

74a. A Guernsey kitchen probably at the turn of the century.

74b. A farmhouse at St Saviour's dated 1912-13.

75. Accused of erecting a stable using materials acquired from the Germans during the Occupation, Albert Chick, of Nelville, Les Dunes, Castel, was sent to prison for six months. The stable was also used as a venue for private parties and one night 53 people were discovered there by a German patrol and were forced to remain there all night. When Mr. Chick was released from jail and returned home, on 12 July 1943, he found this simple florally decorated sign awaiting him. It had been painted on a piece of greenhouse glass by Myrtle Le Page (now Mrs. G. E. Tolcher) who worked for Grut's as an artist.

76. In the aftermath of the German Occupation, this barge which had been commandeered by the Germans was left sunk in the Careening Hard. Photograph by L. R. Cohen.

77. During the summer of 1937 someone started a fire inside the chamber of Le Trépied dolmen at Le Catioroc, St Saviour's. As a result, the northernmost of the three capstones collapsed into positions 'X X'. The original position of the capstone is indicated by the dotted line.

78. On 17 January 1974 a massive rescue operation was launched to find the survivors of the crew from the Cypriot motor vessel *Prosperity*, which ran aground on La Conchée reef, Perelle, the previous night. With winds gusting to hurricane force the ship's engine had broken down. None of the 18 crew were recovered alive. The ship broke into two pieces and the cargo of 4,000 cubic metres of timber was soon washed ashore and recovered by islanders. The photograph, taken by Eric Sirett, shows masses of timber at the foot of the 300-ft. cliff at Petit Port. On 11 September 1975, a memorial stone to the victims of the disaster was unveiled at L'Erée by the Guernsey Merchant Navy Association.

79. Building work on the French Halles was started in 1780 and it opened in 1782. In 1886 the present entrance and foyer to the Guille-Allès Library was built. Adjacent at the time was J. Parsons, florist and seedsman, and a post office.

80. So desperate was Major L. Palmer to reach Alderney from Guernsey to see his wife in February 1940, that he posted himself there. All passages in the motor vessel *Joybell III* were booked but, bearing a label 'On His Majesty's Service. Official Paid. Harbourmaster Alderney', it fell to postman Joseph 'Jock' Clark of New Road, St Sampson's to set out 'on the strangest job of his career'. As the pair boarded the vessel Captain James Ingrouille claimed the 'parcel' was not a parcel and he would not take more than 12 passengers. As it happened only 10 passengers turned up. In addition to the postage, the trip cost Major Palmer 'a Guinea or more'. Postman Clark's son, Eric, of Altrincham, Cheshire, supplied this information.

Road Wells and Pumps

Before the first Guernsey Waterworks Company started to supply piped water in 1890, the island's population was below 40,000 and relied entirely on water drawn from wells, streams, quarries and what fell from the sky onto roof tops and filled cisterns. The ancient method of obtaining 'sweet' water from deep inside the earth was practised in Biblical times and well sinking is certainly one of the most ancient of engineering operations. Water from wells is still a vital means of survival in many parts of the world.

Long before Christianity, wells, fountains, springs and pools were worshipped because of their supposed mysterious powers and life-giving properties. In Guernsey and elsewhere some of these waters were thought to alleviate certain ailments. However, there was a changed attitude towards water after the arrival of Christianity. As one historian put it: 'The well before had a spirit; it now had a guardian angel'.

Whenever water was sought, a water diviner – whose powers are still considered somewhat mysterious – was called in to determine the best spot to dig for water. In some places it bubbled from the earth or oozed into a pool. These areas were simply surrounded with protective walls and given a roof and a door. When the intention was to build a dwelling, water was sought below ground and, when found in sufficient quantity, building went ahead. A well might be deep or shallow and often went through rock. Lateral tunnels were sometimes dug which fed into the main shaft.

The well head was usually D-shaped with the flat side facing north to shade it from the sun. Hundreds of these wells are still to be seen: either free-standing near farmhouses and cottages or completely hidden beneath additions to buildings. Many other wells can be seen isolated in fields. These were sunk to supply water to cattle and were provided with stone troughs. With some variations, all served the same purpose: to supply good spring water for drinking, washing or watering animals. The thick circular wall of each well was carefully built and capped over with enormous slabs of stone. In front there was a high stone step and above this a specially designed door with iron hinges.

Water was drawn up in buckets by hand by means of a primitive but effective windlass which spanned the well head. It consisted merely of a peeled tree log with an iron pin at each end. Each pin was inserted into another hard piece of wood or into a stone. The log was drilled to take wooden spokes which enabled the user to turn it by hand to lower and raise the bucket attached to the end of the rope.

During the latter half of the 18th century, hand pumps started to be used. These were placed alongside a well or against a wall. The earliest discovered is dated 1759. When some farmhouses were enlarged wells and pumps were often totally covered. Most of these pumps bear a date and the initials of the owners, neatly cast in lead. However, many of these pumps have been 'rescued' from their original positions and installed as ornamental features elsewhere in the island.

The vast majority of lead-fronted pumps date from the 19th century and many occur well beyond 1890, when piped public water supplies commenced. Indeed, St Peter Port has many pumps with 20th-century dates. This survey is but a small sample of decorated and dated pump heads and wells which can be seen throughout the island. A great number of lead pumps have not only been re-located but have gone to the scrap yard or have been melted down and recycled into fishermen's sinkers: a rather ignominious end to a precious part of our heritage.

If any form of exterior lettering, dating or decoration was required on a pump it was usually a plumber's job to apply his skill according to the customer's requirements. Plumbers could choose a variety of decorative items from a catalogue: double-headed birds; an eagle about to alight on a nest or one in flight. There was a choice of angelic cherubs, emblematic lions or just a lion's head. There were also birds with reptilian features, or flowers, often roses.

The Prince of Wales' feathers was another favourite as was the fleur-de-lys, in a variety of forms. The scallop shell in various forms features prominently on some boxes, especially the early ones. This symbol was commonly worn by pilgrims to religious shrines and is particularly associated with St James of Compostella, in north-west Spain.

Everything suggests that many of these decorations were derived from heraldic devices which date back to the Third Crusade (1139-92). Few St Peter Port pumps bear decoration; most are dominated by the names of the constables. None of the pumps seen bear any decorative reference to the island's way of life.

In many cases pump plaques are unembellished and simply bear the owners' initials and a date indicating when the pump was installed. Initials were usually those of the couple who first owned or built the property. Plumbers known to have cast these plaques in local workshops were: Wyatt and Co., New Street; Wilson, South Esplanade; E. J. Honey, The Bridge, St Sampson's; A. O. Hamon, St Martin's.

In the late 19th century piped water was non-existent in St Peter Port. Water from roof tops was collected in butts and used for washing, bathing and flushing the lavatory. Water required for cooking and drinking had to be fetched from one of the many public pumps, provided by the parish. Some of these are still functional and used in times of drought.

In the days when there were hundreds of small farms, parish authorities built *abreuvoirs*, or drinking places for cattle. These were often adjacent to a shallow well where nearby inhabitants, without their own wells, could draw water. One splendid *abreuvoir* is in St Andrew's, on the border with St Saviour's, just off La Villiaze Road. Here is a paved area leading down to a water trough and nearby well. This sylvan setting can be reached from two directions. In 1899, the Paroise de St André saw fit to erect a blue-granite stone of monumental proportions to indicate the spot. The stone may have been originally intended as a churchyard memorial but now stands at the entrance to a humble trough and fountain, which is seldom used.

With the gradual introduction of piped water throughout the island, the use of well water declined. However, farmers who also combined their activities with horticulture continued to use 'free' water from their own wells. Hundreds of windmills were installed which raised water into elevated tanks which provided the necessary pressure. When stone quarrying left scars and large holes in the landscape, these quickly filled with water and became reservoirs from which owners could draw or sell supplies.

Petrol and oil driven pumps as well as electric pumps replaced those driven by the wind and there is now almost nothing left of the spindly towers of mills which so efficiently extracted water from the earth. There are still many diehards, however, who for economic or other reasons use well water for both domestic and commercial purposes.

The standard diameter for a well shaft was eight feet, which continued to the bottom. In some cases the excavation was aided by the use of explosives. The shaft was lined with dry stones about two feet thick, starting at the bottom. The builder would walk round in a circle, laying stones as he went. When finished, the resulting hole was built up in masonry in a variety of forms. Wells were capped over and pumps fitted. These are usually dated and the majority are from the 19th century. Finely worked public fountains were also built as part of the harbour works and remain as splendid examples of the stonemason's art.

Most of the privately owned wells and pumps in the country also had large stone troughs placed adjacent to them. Some of these are of enormous proportions and there is no certainty they were all made locally. Many are thought to have been imported as ships' ballast and probably came from Normandy. However, old quarrymen used to talk about 'taking out a trough', which was a long, arduous and sometimes dangerous task. Very much later in this century at Le Couteur's Granite Works at Rocquaine, a few troughs were made using mechanical means. In the 1990s little granite was being quarried in Guernsey and some was being imported from Brittany. Troughs of all sizes were also being shipped in from Normandy for use as garden ornaments.

A large number of troughs are to be seen in their original positions. Regrettably, perhaps, such is the antique value placed on them that great numbers have been removed, others have been spirited away from isolated fields and have completely vanished.

Assuming some of the earliest wells were close to farmhouses, often in the yard near the front door, they were very substantially built above ground. The material used was often found on the spot or quarried from nearby. The well at La Houguette, Castel, which is in front of the house, stands 76 in. high, being 68 in. wide and 55 in. from front to back. The cap-stone is in one piece of blue-granite and the doorstep is one piece of Cobo granite, as is the rest of the construction. On each side of the door is a ledge upon which a bucket could be rested. Adjacent is a red-granite trough, beside which is a flat blue stone set at a slight angle. When clothes were washed out of doors, this stone was used as a 'washing board'.

Before the States Water Board was established in 1920 and the water undertaking became 'nationalised', two companies had sought to supply the island needs. The first was approved by the States in 1887 and it sank a 50-ft. well just west of St Saviour's reservoir and piped water to its main reservoir in the Steam Mill Lanes to provide domestic supplies to St Peter Port in 1889. The system was officially opened in 1890.

In 1893 the first Guernsey Waterworks Company was unable to continue and the second Guernsey Waterworks Company Ltd. came into being. It abandoned the St Saviour's well and sank seven wells on the highest land in the south of the island. The official opening of the company's operation was on 9 May 1895 and the main was extended to St Sampson's. It was only when the demand for water became so great after the First World War that the States took over the undertaking.

Meanwhile public pumps in St Peter Port and elsewhere continued to be used until water mains extended to all parts of the island. The greatest concentration of pumps was in St Peter Port, and while the majority of these were regrettably allowed to deteriorate or have completely vanished, some attempt was made in the late 1980s to rescue and refurbish a few of them and present them as antique street furniture. The town douzaine were slow to do this as already many of the country parishes had seen fit to preserve and maintain their pumps and *abreuvoirs* with great pride over a long period of time.

In the country, where farms were once numerous and herds small in number, farmers tethered each animal. In the process of moving a herd from field to field, six or so cows might be taken to an *abreuvoir* for watering. In the 18th century hundreds of wells were sunk in fields to provide water on the spot. As with domestic wells, these had adjacent granite troughs from which the cows could drink. Field well building went on for 80 or 90 years but many were unsuccessful and dried up.

To save expense, where two properties joined, one well was often sunk which was fitted with a door on each side. There are a number of jointly owned wells in fields and elsewhere. Sometimes, according to T. F. Priaulx, a clause was inserted in a contract of sale, relating to *droits de puissage* and many quarrels have arisen between owners of adjoining properties over alleged rights to draw water from wells. On 25 October 1778, Nicholas de Garis of Les Grandes Moulins wrote in his journal: 'We started to sink a well at Les Hougues (Castel) and finished it 30 March 1780. It is between Sieur Pierre Naftel and me, Nicholas de Garis'. This well, with two openings, stands in the hedge between the two fields they owned.

Field wells are now seldom used and many are completely overgrown and quite invisible. Nowadays farmers tow water tankers to their fields to fill old bath tubs from which cattle can drink at will, as they are no longer tethered.

Wells have been discovered in unlikely places. In an old cottage at St Saviour's one was found below the floor boards in the sitting room. It belonged to a former cottage over which the 'new' cottage had been built a century or more later. At the rope walk, St John's, a deep well was discovered below a slab near the front of the former rope works. The water had been used by the rope makers to wet the strands of rope as it was being made.

Finally, we should never underestimate the power of water. When a shallow well was in use outside a St Martin's house after the last war, the owner believed that by stopping the overflow he would have more water in his well. Instead, it forced its way underground and emerged as a 'lake' in the kitchen.

St Pierre du Bois

81. Mrs. Annie de Garis drawing water from her well at La Cité, a cottage at Route de Canteraine, St Pierre du Bois, when it was in use about 1900. Today water from it is pumped automatically. It is, however, still equipped with a windlass. Photograph by F. W. Guerin.

82. Mr. W. Torode watering his cows at the *abreuvoir* at La Vallée, St Pierre du Bois, *c.*1958. These places, which are to be seen all over the island, are no longer used. Photograph by S. M. Henry.

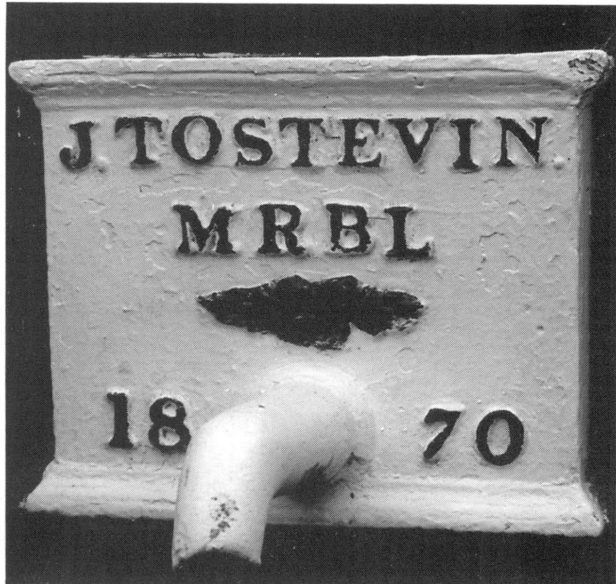

3. *(Above)* This pump stands
 the yard at La Houguette,
es Adams, St Pierre du Bois.
ated 1818, it has a rather coy-
oking lion dormant. The
itials 'IRB' and 'MBA'
dicate it was the home of Jean
obin and Marie Brouard. In
e 1950s the house was still lit
y oil lamps. Part of this
roperty dates back to the late
7th century.

4. *(Above right)* This pump
tands in the yard at La
Couture, Les Paysans, St Pierre
u Bois. Dated 1870 and well
ared for, the initials 'MRBL'
epresent Mary Robilliard.

5. *(Right)* Until 1977 this
omplete field well with
vindlass and iron winding
andle was still in use at Val des
Paysans. The ivy and other
rowth on this and other wells
elps to keep it intact.

St Saviour's

86a. The parish pump at Bas Rouvets, St Saviour's is dated 1885. It backs onto a wall and cattle trough.

86b. Very few islanders still draw water from public wells. Marguerite de Garis is one and she uses the water at Bas Rouvets for drinking.

87. A field well and trough off Rue St Pierre, St Saviour's. Granite troughs such as this large one may be of French origin. It is thought many were brought here from the continent as ships' ballast.

88. The lead pump box which stood above the well at Primrose Farm, St Saviour's is dated 1831 and bears a pair of winged gryphons with lions' legs and a short tail as well as a pair of birds in flight.

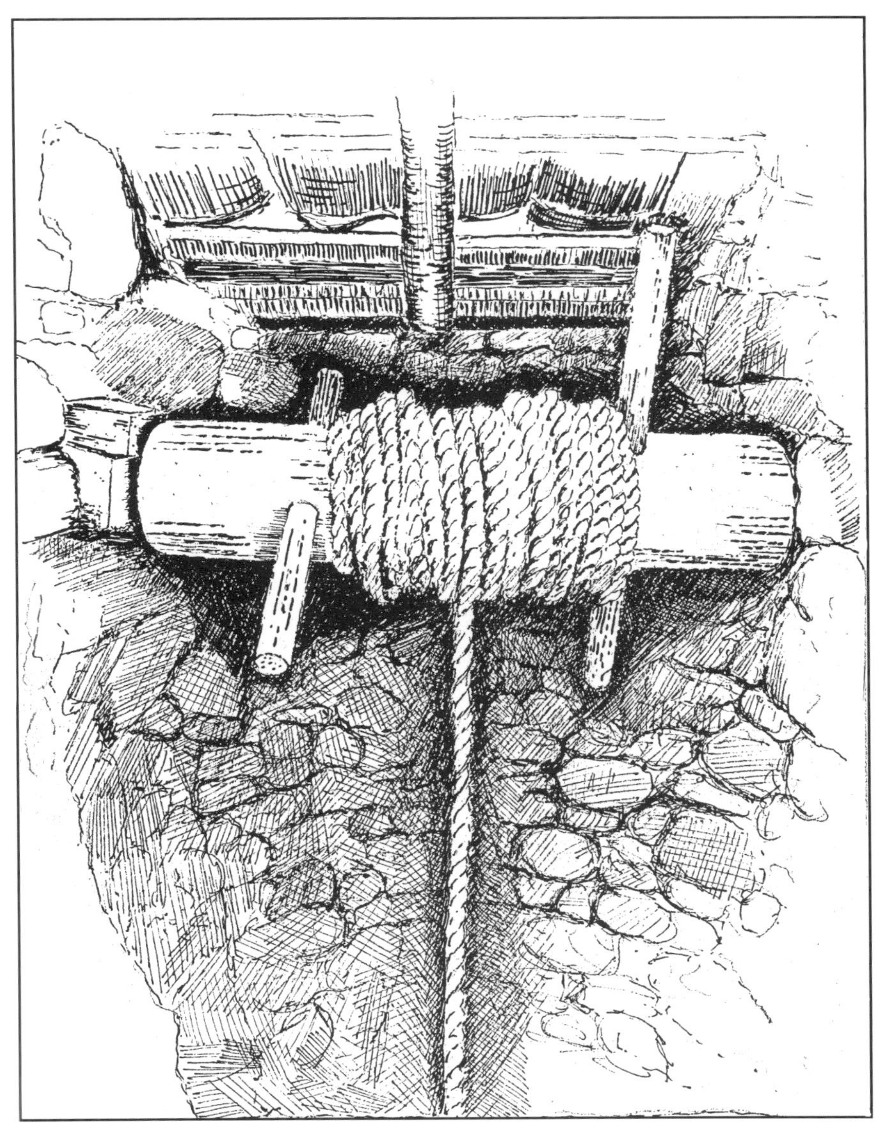

89. The windlass above the well at La Belial, Rue du Belial, St Saviour's. It has a pantiled roof and stands at the rear of the 18th-century cottage.

St Andrew's

90. About 10 years after a St Andrew's parish pump was stolen from over the 60-ft. deep well at Courtil Ronchin, another had been acquired and installed by the douzaine. It came from a farmhouse at La Ramée, St Peter Port. Dated 1804 it bears the initials A. B. H. In 1985 the pump was reinstated. Standing beside it *(left to right)* are Ivan Robert (Constable), Deputy Jean Pritchard, John Bougourd, who made the wooden case, and Douzenier Denzil La Farge.

91. An unusually decorated lead-fronted pump box dated 1881, found at St Sampson's and now at St Andrew's.

92. This monumental stone indicates the location of a St Andrew's parish watering place for cattle. It is near the boundary with St Saviour's parish at La Villiaze.

Castel

93. At La Houguette, Castel, is a splendid example of a farm well. It is 76 in. high and built of Cobo granite. Beside the stone trough is a large flat stone used as a 'washing board'.

94. The 'curative' well at St George, Castel. It became widely known that the water from this and other wells would cure *le mal d'la Faöntoine*, the so-called well disease, a swelling above the instep or the hands and arms. It was also said that if barren women came here on nine successive mornings and drank the water, a cure would be affected. When Christianity was established, these practices were frowned upon by the Church and a symbolic cross was placed on the well. During the 15th century it apparently became the haunt of 'shady characters' and in 1408 the Royal Court passed an Act making the path to the well open only to the faithful and the sick.

95. A lion dormant and the heads of four other lions appear on this pump dated 1818 which can be seen *in situ* over a concrete trough at the Folk Museum at Saumarez Park, Castel.

96. The farm well at Le Tertre, Castel, home of Peter Girard.

97. Was the word 'hopital' deliberately spelt without an 's' in order to find space for it? If not, then why did the word, which is cast in lead, not bear a circumflex accent? The 1810 dated pump stands in the yard of the institution. It was restored and given a new box in 1991 by the maintenance staff.

Torteval

98. Parish pump, well and trough at Route des Laurens, Torteval. One of four modern iron pumps in the parish for public use.

Vale

99. At Hocart's Farm, Rue de Bas, Vale, is a good example of a wooden case pump standing against a wall of a recessed area in front of a farm building. Dated 1869, it feeds into a large granite trough. Another similar pump is in a garden on the opposite side of the wall.

100. The initials on this pump of 1823 stand for Thomas Ogier. The pump stands in the yard at Le Tertre, Vale, and is embellished with fleur-de-lys, winged beasts and lions' heads.

101. A cottage at Les Grippios de Bas, near Bordeaux, Vale, has this well, which is complete with windlass and door.

102. At the cottage known as 'Two Wells', Old Marais, Vale, water from this hooded well is drawn automatically for domestic use and is also a pleasing feature of the garden.

St Sampson's

103. This is thought to be the one remaining public pump in St Sampson's parish. It stood in an unnamed lane off the Vale Road and was rescued by the parish constables and douzaine. A new wooden case was made in the prison workshop and the pump now stands at the Douzaine Room, Le Murier. This parish had no public water supply for drinking or fire fighting until 1862, when underground cisterns were built and fed from nearby quarries.

104. In an overgrown, quite rustic setting stands this well and trough at Les Grandes Maisons Road, St Sampson's.

Forest

105. The free-standing parish case pump at Le Bourg, Forest, dated 1831. The lead front bears a pair of lions' heads, three rosettes and a horizontal key. It was restored in 1974.

106. A restored windmill for pumping water at Les Houards farm, Forest. As well as Chas. P. Kinnell, another firm who erected windmills was Thorne and Co., South Esplanade. The company advertised: 'A feature of Guernsey is The Windmills! What are they doing? Saving money for the users.'

107. No more than a hole in the wall, this small public well is at Le Cas Rouge, near Le Bigard, Forest.

108. A small, shallow well at Chasse des Galliennes, Le Bigard, Forest.

St Martin's

109. This postcard view of the 'wishing well' at La Ville Amphrey, St Martin's was taken *c.*1906. Of the three children coming down the lane, the one on the right is Grace Clark, who was born in 1899. She is now Mrs. Ollivier and at the age of 91 was able to name the three women standing facing the camera as *(left to right)* Gladys Thoume, Rita Rose (later to become Mrs. Brehaut) and Edith Rose, who married Arthur Stevens, who for many years was the engineer on the R. N. L. I. lifeboat *Queen Victoria*, stationed at St Peter Port.

110. Well and trough at Saints Road, St Martin's, which is shared by two properties.

111. Les Maindonneaux, as part of the Bon Air estate, St Martin's, belonged to Daniel de Lisle Brock, Bailiff of Guernsey from 1821 to 1842. Mrs. Adolphus Carey lived at Bon Air in 1874. The estate was acquired by Frederick Mansell Allès, one of the founders of the Guille-Allès Library. The pump, cast in lead, has a bronze tap, bears his name and the date 1885.

112. A paved *abreuvoir* built into a bank at Le Becquet, St Martin's.

113. Public well and *abreuvoir* at La Fosse, St Martin's.

St Peter Port

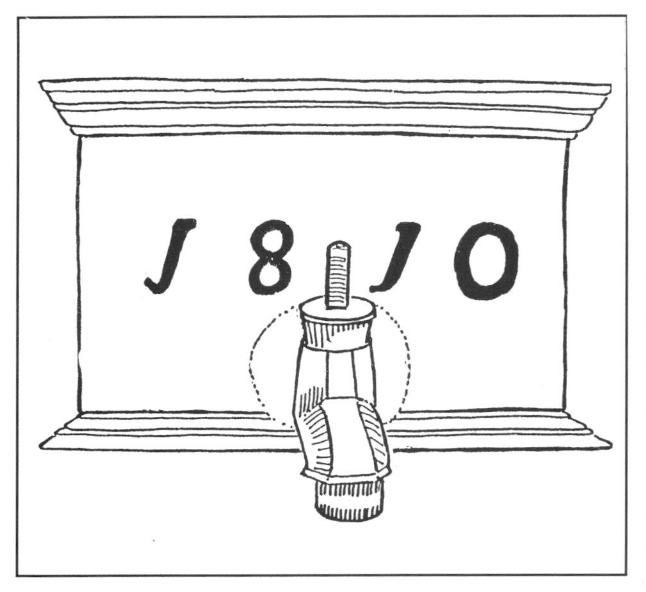

114. *(Above left)* Pump box dated 1810 at the former States Prison, St James' Street. Originally H.M. Prison, it was built in 1811 at a cost of £11,000. The prison was closed in 1990, when a new one was built.

115. *(Above)* In 1770 the pump at the foot of College Street was attached to the master's house of Elizabeth College. It became a public pump in 1831 and was renovated as late as 1972 when the depth of water was 30 ft. St Peter Port constables sank wells and constructed pumps between *c.*1784 until at least 1887. Many of the dates merely indicate when the pump was refurbished.

116. *(Left)* In 1789 the *chefs de famille* of St Peter Port authorised Constable Bonamy to purchase a pump and piece of land at the foot of Le Marchant Street for the price of £400 sterling, it being stipulated that 'no dressing of fish or washing of clothes' be permitted. The pump was overhauled in 1971 and the depth of water was 60 ft. It is probably the best preserved of the town pumps as it is complete with two D-shaped troughs to catch the drips and provide drinking water for the dogs. Attached to the spout is a bucket hook.

117a. This free standing pump at Cambridge Park guards a 48-ft. deep well. It has an outstanding lion's head spout and an ornamental granite finial which is rather out of proportion to the pump. The enormous weight of this piece of stone must have been the reason for the thick iron case upon which it stands. The plaque bears the inscription: St Pierre Port. C. Vaucour, J. H. Guilbert, Constables, 1873.

7b. The plaque and inscription on the pump at Cambridge Park cast in iron.

118. In 1837, 22 householders petitioned the Constables of St Peter Port to erect a pump in the Pollet, as the one in Smith Street was 'often dry' and they had to go as far as Church Square. The land was donated in 1839 and a pump erected. When overhauled in 1971 the well had a depth of 22 ft.

119. Candie House (*c*.1780), which is now known as the Priaulx Library, was originally owned by Peter Mourant, whose initials are to be seen on the pump box in the back yard, together with the date 1817. It also bears a pair of scallop shells and an eagle alighting on a nest. Mourant sold the house to Joshua Priaulx and it was then leased to Peter Stafford Carey (later to become Sir Peter), Bailiff from 1845-83, who lived there for 40 years. It was then purchased by Osmond de Beauvoir Priaulx from his brother, who made it over as a gift to the States in 1871. Standing in Candie Gardens – once the garden of Candie House – is a greenhouse built for Peter Mourant in 1792 or 1793. It is the first to have been built on the island.

120. The front of a typical pump in St Peter Port. Dated 1893, it is dominated with the names of *les connétables* and stands in a recess in Mount Row. It is one of several which have been refurbished.

121. An extremely good example of a 'restored' pump is outside Raglan House, The Queen's Road, St Peter Port. Bearing the date 1824, it is also decorated with a pair of fleur-de-lys, an eagle with outstretched wings alighting on a nest, a floral decoration and a beautiful sunburst surrounding the spout. This is a public pump which has lost its wooden outer casing.

122. In the garden of Colborne Place, The Queen's Road, St Peter Port, stands this monumental pump on a granite plinth, surrounded with flagstones. Information inside the wooden box indicates that the pump was cast in lead by Charles Andros in 1835. The well was then 59 ft. deep. In 1929, when it was measured, the depth of water was 17 ft. The pipe into the well was renewed on 28 June 1934 by H. Wood, S. Chutter and H. Loesby. The present owner, R. W. Bowden, restored the timber work in 1974, when it was also repainted.

123. Still in use at Trinity Square is this iron double-sided pump. The spout from the lion's head feeds the horse trough and on the left is the tap and bucket hook for domestic users. A warning notice above cautions against using the water unless it is boiled.

Men of the Sea

124a. Among the fishermen of Port Grat, Rousse and Grand Havre who braved a storm to help rescue 43 survivors of a shipwreck were George Bewey, Adolphus Gaudion, Desiré Quentin and another fisherman. The stricken ship was the *S.S. Channel Queen*, a twin screw steamship of 125 ft. built in 1895, which struck Les Roches Noires, a mile-and-half offshore on 1 February 1898. Many others assisted at five o'clock that morning. The 21 men in this photograph took part. Those saved were succoured by such people as Thomas H. Henry and his wife, of Les Vardes. Among the survivors were two women and numerous Bretons on their way home to France from England, where they had been selling onions. In addition to the passengers there was a crew of eighteen. A memorial to the ten who died in the disaster can be seen at St Sampson's churchyard. The photograph was taken at Les Vardes farm.

124b. This 20 in. long bronze fish ornament was recovered from the wreck of the *Channel Queen* in the 1960s by diver Richard Tostevin.

124c. The four men in this photograph were presented with medals for their part in the *Channel Queen* rescue. They were *(left to right)* George Bewey, Adolph Gaudion, Desiré Quentin and an unidentified fisherman. The presentations took place at St Julian's hall and the *Try*, one of the boats used in the rescue, was taken to the hall where a dramatic backdrop showing the wreck was set up. One medal was from the French Ministre de la Marine. In addition barometers and clocks were also given to rescuers. The grandson of Admiral Lord de Saumarez, James St Vincent 4th Lord de Saumarez, presented portraits of his grandfather to some of the rescuers as well as £5 each. The photograph was taken by M. J. Cluett and is by courtesy of Gordon Gaudion.

124d. The bell from the *Channel Queen*, dated 1895, was recovered by diver George Head, after it had been on the sea bed for over 60 years.

125. Wilfred Gaudion (1888-1977) was one of a number of fishermen who kept their boats on the Rousse side of Grand Havre. They worked from these moorings each year from about March until the end of October. Others included Walter Bewey (*Shamrock*); Hedley Bewey, senior (*Barbara*); Hedley Bewey, junior (*Ajax*); Stan Bewey (*Mizpah*); Jim Ozanne and his son, Wilburt (*May Queen*); Edwin Gaudion (*Lavis*). The *Lavis* is now owned by Basil Gaudion.

126. Wilf Savident was the last of the full-time fishermen to work out of Perelle and gave up fishing as such in 1991. At the age of 13 he started to go fishing with his father in the boat *Nora*. His own boat, *Joan II*, was built at Poole in 1947. His original boat, *Joan*, was wrecked in a gale.

127. In 1896, the *Wonder* (GU 132) was built at James de Garis' boatyard at Les Vinaires, St Pierre du Bois for the brothers E. H. and T. H. Gaudion of Roncefer, St Sampson's. She was cutter rigged, being 23 ft. long with a beam of 8½ ft. and a depth of five feet. She displaced 5.65 tons and the Gaudions kept her at Grand Havre until 1910, when they acquired the *Pioneer* (*see below*). The *Wonder* then went to Edwin C. Ozanne of Grandes Rocques Barracks and he kept her until the end of 1924 when she was bought by Henry Ashplant of Perelle, where she was kept until the end of 1939 when he sold her to Mr. Budden. In 1946 the Le Page brothers, Jack and Tom, acquired her and made considerable alterations, which included making her longer, giving her a canoe stern and flared bows. After they retired from fishing the *Wonder* went to Jersey in 1977. In 1992 she was returned to Guernsey, where she is being restored by John Cluett.

128. The fishermen brothers Tom and Jack Le Page, seen here together after the Second World War, accompanied Frenchman Xavier Gollivet during the Occupation when the three escaped to France in their boat *Etoile du Marin*. They left on 22 January 1945, taking with them details of German fortifications and plans of minefields, obtained by Gollivet when he worked in the German harbourmaster's office, as well as information concerning the German attack on Granville. The escape was planned by French Consular Agent, M. L. V. Lambert, who also obtained illicit petrol.

The fishermen at Grand Havre were nothing short of amazed when the first motorised fishing boat arrived at her moorings off Rousse in 1909. The spanking new five-ton motor cutter was appropriately named *Pioneer* and given the registration number 16 by H.M.Customs. The boat was a revelation and other fishermen stood in awe and wonder when they saw her in action. She had been built at Poplar, London and was owned by the brothers Edwin and Thomas Gaudion of Roncefer, St Sampson's. She had only a 4 h.p. petrol engine but she could actually punch the tide and motor against the wind, while other fishermen had to rely entirely on the wind and their oars or where the tide took them. Edwin Henri Gaudion was born in 1875 and died in 1932. In 1920 the brothers sold the *Pioneer* to James and Philip Guille of La Rade, Sark, who used her until 1923, when James Guille, who then lived at 3 Sir William Place, St Peter Port, owned her and she was crewed by Tom Hamon and his son, also called Tom. In 1945 she was purchased by Frank H. Le Page; she was licensed to carry 12 passengers and was frequently used to ferry people to and from Sark and Herm as well as for longline fishing and seining for sand-eels. In 1964 she was sold to Robert H. Hudson of Les Jenemies, St Saviour's, who moored her at Perelle. In November 1966, she was severely damaged in a gale and what remained of her was driven ashore on the north side of Lihou Island.

129a. The *Pioneer*, one of the first motorised fishing vessels to be used in Guernsey waters.

129b. After 57 years of service, the end of the *Pioneer* came in 1966.

129c. Frank Le Page, who owned the *Pioneer* between 1945-64.

130. Wilburt Ozanne with a catch of conger at Rousse. He fished for many years with his father, Jim Ozanne, in their boat the *May Queen*.

131. A shark caught off Rousse, Grand Havre in about 1930 by fishermen Edwin Ozanne *(left)* and his brother Jim *(right)*. A tent was erected around it and a small charge made for viewing by the public.

132. It was a laborious process provisioning Les Hanois lighthouse, one-and-a-quarter miles off the south-west of the island in 1934. At that time and for some years after, stores were first loaded onto a box cart at Portelet Harbour and driven into the sea, before being transferred to a small waiting boat. Seen in the bow is Harry de la Mare and sculling the boat is Helier Le Lacheur, both 'regulars' on this monthly run. The loaded boat was then rowed to the motorised fishing vessel *Rival*, anchored offshore, which towed the boat to the lighthouse.

133a. This cottage, at Route de la Maladerie overlooking Perelle, was the home of fisherman Jean Jehan, who owned the 19-ft. fishing boat *Grace Darling* (GU 65), which is the nearest boat in the drawing. She was built at Ogier's yard, St Sampson's and first registered in 1913. As a sailing boat she was rigged with a jib, staysail and mainsail and was used for potting and line fishing. She also took parties to Herm after she was equipped with an engine. This boat is one of the oldest locally built vessels still afloat and is owned by the Hackett family of Les Villets, Forest. The cottage was demolished by the Germans who replaced it with a bunker about 1942-43. The dwelling which now stands near this site is Coin des Pecheurs. From an original photograph by Aline Head.

133b. Harold Roberts, a boat builder from Icart, St Martin's, repaired the keel of the *Grace Darling* in 1972.

134. *Ormonde*, a Guernsey-built boat being launched at St Peter Port in 1927, when she was owned by Peter Kinnersly. Her two previous owners were Geoff Le Cheminant of Grand Havre, Vale and George Savident of Portelet, Torteval.

135. In the spring of 1980 a beacon was erected by the States on rocks known as La Mare de la Greve, Perelle. Seen from left to right: Ross Ferbrache, M. Le Lacheur, Gordon Ferbrache, Edwin Martel and Johnny Mallett.

136. The west coast of the island was the last place still to be used by seaweed burners. This picture taken in the 1960s shows Bertie J. Le Lacheur and Douglas Robilliard at work on a beach near Le Douit du Moulin, Rocquaine. The ash from the burned weed was used as a fertiliser.

137. Frederick Brehaut was known as 'Seaweed Joe'. He collected dry *vraic* at Perelle and used it as fuel in his hearth. He also sold the ash to tomato growers.

138. Art Le Page, a St Peter Port fisherman who made *poniers-à-co* (fish baskets) when he was no longer able to go to sea.

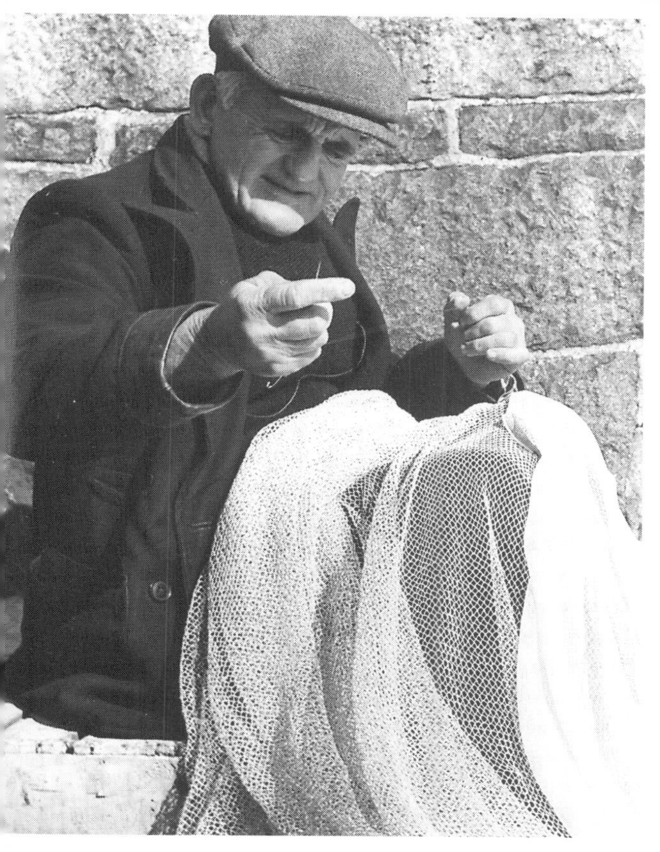

139. St Peter Port fisherman Eddie Down mending a seine net on the Albert Dock slipway about 1965. The Down brothers fished in their boat *Smilax*, mainly for whiting (otherwise pollock). Traditionally, sand-eels for bait were caught by their thousand off the sandy bays on the east coast of Herm.

140. Adolphus Saunders was one of three, perhaps four full-time fishermen at Saints Harbour before and after the Second World War. He lived in a cottage at Icart Point and is seen here making a crabpot. Two other fishermen at Saints Harbour were Billy Saunders and Ned Waldron. During the winter, when fishing was not possible, Adolphus fattened steers on the cliffs which he exported to Reading market.

141. The chosen calling of Bill Domaille was fishing. He lived at Chouet, Vale and was a philosophical man and a loner. He owned many boats and experimented with many operating methods. A daring seaman in his youth, he could 'read' the sea and knew the rocky coast around the island by heart. He would pass between narrow gaps in rocks, where no one else would dare go, just for fun. His friends at sea were the gulls who perched on a special platform to be fed. He once owned a Guernsey-built schooner and said '... a boat's not alive unless she's sailing'.

142a. The inshore Guernsey fishing boat of the last century and well into this was often no more than 13 ft. long. Many were built at Les Vinaires, St Pierre du Bois, or at a boat-yard at Rue de la Vallée, Torteval. Inside this half model is some rare information giving details of names of fishermen for whom a boat was built. It reads: 'Modelle du Bateau des Sr Corbin 1866; A du Batau A. de la Mare du douit 1866; A du Bato de Daniel Ozanne Castel 1868; A du Bato de William Jehan St Sav 1871; A du Batau Pour Serks de 13 pids en 1881'.

142b. Models of two basic types of Guernsey fishing boat: the shallow draught inshore boat used for potting and line fishing and the deep keeled type employed for mackerel drifting and other deep sea work.

143. Captain Fred Noyon, S.G.M. (1879-1962), who became a fisherman, pilot and master mariner and was awarded Lloyd's Sea Gallantry Medal for rescuing the crew of a ship which had gone aground in the Thames estuary. During the Occupation he and Bill Endicott escaped from Guernsey in his fishing boat *Littlewood* on 3 November 1944. They took with them information about the dire state of the island's food supplies as well as details about the German defences. They finally reached London on 12 November.

144. Bec du Nez, on the island's east coast, lies tucked between Fermain and St Martin's Point. The fishermen's hut there looked like this when it was sketched by the author in 1939. It shows conger hanging to dry for bait, willow pots and a *courge* – the cigar-shaped wicker baskets hanging in the doorway and lying in the foreground. Live sand-eels were put into these baskets, towed behind boats and used for bait.

145a. One of the outstanding fishermen operating from Bec du Nez before the last war was Charlie Luscombe. Not only did he make all his crabpots but he built boats, including his own. One is the 17-ft. *Janet II*, built in 1927 and still afloat. Much of the wood used was Guernsey-grown elm from trees which once grew along Sausmarez Road, St Martin's.

145b. *Janet II* with Joe Leaman, Charlie Luscombe and Joe's son, Dick, on board off Bec du Nez in about 1936.

146. Harry Smith was also a full-time fisherman at Bec du Nez and the last of the pre-war men to use an open rowing boat, which was a mere 12 ft. in length.

147. Joe Leaman was another fisherman at Bec du Nez in the 1920s and 1930s. His boat, the *Hope*, was only 13½ ft. in length. He is seen here baiting a pot off St Martin's Point.

148a. In the past, unlike today, old boats which were no longer seaworthy were put to good use and given another lease of life by being used as sheds. For many years before the war this old upturned boat was at the Castle Emplacement, St Peter Port, where it was used as a fisherman's store.

148b. The upturned boat in this picture taken in Sark was raised with thatched sides to give it headroom. It was probably used as a small stable. It is covered with fishermen's rope and cork floats.

149. The 21 ft. *Morning Star*, built by Laurie Roberts in Sark for Miss Sylvia Lamb in 1950. The vessel is seen here, having been taken from the boatyard at the north end of the island coming down the steep Harbour Hill to the Creux Harbour. This vessel is now in Guernsey.

150. The *Challenger* (GU 221), a fishing boat owned by Len Langlois, who is seen standing in the stern. The photograph was taken in 1966.

151. In the early 19th century sailors often mistook Guernsey for the Scillies. Local mariner Alexander Deschamps, who was St Peter Port harbourmaster in the 19th century, published his sailing directions to the island in 1806. He advised mariners not to attempt to enter St Sampson's harbour unless their ship was sinking! He mentioned one of two beacons, one being Jack the Sailor, and cautioned: '... mind the tide and have always an eye on Bréhon and Jethou; take care to enter correctly, these marks are very quick, but excellent and plain'. In 1990 a £9.75 million reclamation scheme of the area near the beacon started and in 1991 the beacon was removed. Jack the Sailor beacon stood on Grunette rock east of the south arm of St Sampson's breakwater before the area was reclaimed.

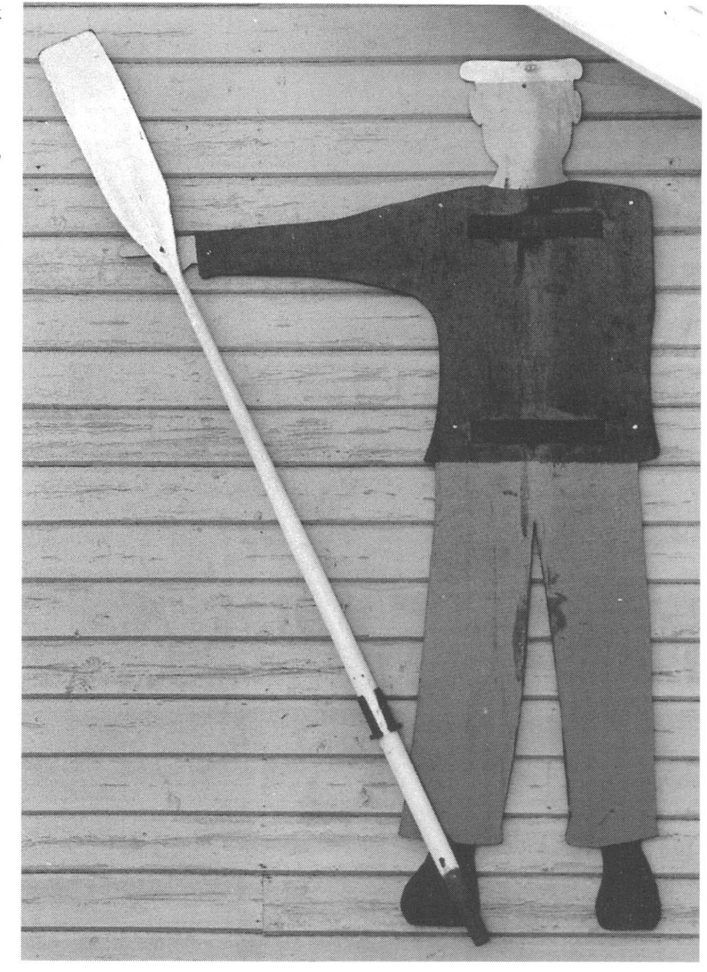

151b. With the addition of an oar, the old beacon is now the mascot of the Guernsey Rowing Club.

Guernsey Places

152. As long ago as 1786 a watchtower stood on the high ground at Le Becquet de Fermain on the St Peter Port side of the bay of that name. It was removed in 1815 and replaced by this sentry box which is commonly called the Pepper Pot. As a sea mark it was also called Le Cocquelin because of its resemblance to a seashell. When England was at war with France this area was heavily defended, a stone bulwark being built across the bay inside which was Battery North and Battery South. The gunpowder magazine behind the present tower has long been a tea-room.

153. The ancient house at Les Beaucamps, Castel, as it looked in 1954. The house was later demolished and the arch was rebuilt into a new house, Le Merlin at Rue du Hurel, Torteval in 1966. It was built on the lines of a traditional Guernsey farmhouse.

154a. Between 1787 and 1807, when the Braye du Valle waterway was drained and became part of 'Greater Guernsey', the Grand Pont connecting St Sampson's South Side with what we now call the North Side, ended on a mudflat. At high water the sea entered every creek, including part of that which is now the Vale Avenue. The building on the left, which became Leale's Ltd., ironmongers, came well after the reclamation was complete. The long house facing the camera stood isolated on la Hougue du Valle in the Clos du Valle and outcrops of rock in front of it are to be clearly seen in this picture which was taken in about 1880. Access to the dwelling, known then as the *Ship Inn*, which belonged to the Gillingham family, and later as Rockmount Restaurant, was via the Hougue du Valle Lane.

N
Clos du Valle
Braye du Valle
Hougue du Valle
South Side

1. Braye Road
2. Rt. des Coutures
3. Summerfield Rd.
4. Ship Inn
5. Grand Pont

154b. This sketch map, after William Gardner's 1787 survey of Guernsey, shows the location of the former *Ship Inn* at the Hougue du Valle.

154c. When the east end of the old building was demolished it made way for the cutting of the Vale Avenue. Louis R. Cohen took this photograph for the *Guernsey Society Journal* in 1953 when Leale's was selling petrol from a pump on the corner and Cross and Co. had a furniture shop opposite. Parking was no problem in those days and there were no apparent yellow or white lines in sight, let alone a roundabout.

154d. In 1965 the former restaurant building was purchased by Mr. and Mrs. A. D. Martel. The Martel family had been running Martel's Stores at Delancey since 1919 and were well-known for their mobile shops, which were to be seen in all parts of the island. A new building was erected in front of the old and opened in 1966 and this is what we see today. The stores closed in 1975.

155a. Le Moulin de Cantereine was the last of the island's water mills to work. This shows the complete complex at St Pierre du Bois in 1925. The wheel and works fell into complete disrepair after being used by the Germans during the Occupation. The property was left to the National Trust of Guernsey by Elizabeth Silton in 1989, and the wheel was rebuilt and restored to working order in 1991 by students at the College of Further Education.

155b. The Cantereine mill complex in 1925.

156. This carving of a barque is on the back door of the farmhouse, La Mare, St Pierre du Bois. Below are the initials 'NLM' (Nicholas Le Messurier). Nicholas was a sea captain who traded in the West Indies and is known to have painted pictures. He died in 1884 aged thirty-seven. A pump in the oldest part of the house is dated 1770 and is initialled 'PLM' (Peter Le Messurier).

157. Supporting the gallery of Victoria Tower, whose foundation stone was laid by Major-General John Bell, Lieutenant-Governor, on 2 April 1848, are eight granite corbels. Contractors for the building were Matthieu and Jacques Tostevin. This sculpted wooden corbel was used as a model for all eight. It was made in 1847 and was partly burned in a fire in 1935. The tower is 96 ft. high and cost £2,000.

158. A pillar outside the former blacksmith's forge at the junction between Rue des Caches and Rue Cauchée, St Martin's, bears the inscription 'DBH 1827'. It stands for Daniel Brehaut who owned the property in the early 1800s, when the forge was in use. An apprentice who worked there married a daughter of Daniel Brehaut and emigrated to Australia in the 1850s. The picture dates from 1855.

159. Shoeing forges abounded well into the 20th century. According to *Hill's Directory* of 1874 this one at Le Coudré, St Pierre du Bois, was run by Nicholas Bourgaise.

160. The Guille-Allès Library was first established in 1856 and moved to the Market Square in 1882. On 27 March 1895, the Artisans' Institute was opened and was 'intended exclusively for the use and benefit of the working class of the island – men and women'. The building was formerly *Coles' Farmers' Hotel*. This photograph dates from *c*.1958 and was taken by S. M. Henry.

161. This early photograph looking up Guelles Road, St Peter Port shows a roadsweeper with his wheelbarrow, a small boy with a hoop, a milkman with a small handcart and a pony and trap coming down the hill driven by a bowler-hatted man. The photograph was taken by Aline Head, *c*.1900.

162. Fort Le Crocq, St Saviour's, as it was seen by a Miss de Putron who painted it in about 1890. In 1932, the disused fort was purchased by Mr. and Mrs. Harold Le Parmentier, who were the first to install a swimming pool in the island, into which sea water was pumped by the fire brigade. When the Germans evicted the owners during the Occupation, the fort was totally destroyed. However, shortly after the War it was rebuilt as a residence by Mr. and Mrs. John Van Draege.

163. The north side of Fort Saumarez, beside the present slipway to the beach, looked like this before German forces built Hitler's Atlantic Wall along Guernsey's west coast in about 1942. These buildings were directly below the martello tower built in 1804, which the Germans heightened and converted into a naval observation tower and direction finding post. A searchlight bunker was also installed.

164. Supplies of running water for domestic use in St Peter Port started after 1890, when the first Waterworks Company laid a main from a 50-ft. well west of St Saviour's reservoir to one in the Steam Mill Lanes. Water from this also fed a number of public fountains, including this one at La Petite Fontaine, off Victoria Road. The picture shows two well-dressed boys, one of whom has taken water from the gushing stream.

65. This photograph by Aline Head shows part of Mansell Court, where John Henry Shayer had his tinsmith's shop and Mathias D. Hawke had his 'co-operative drug store', according to *Kelly's Directory* of 1899. Mr. Hawke also sold tobacco, cigars, toilet soap and perfumes. Hereabouts also were a grocer, draper, hairdresser, sanitary engineer, ironmonger, two bakeries, a butcher and a slipper manufacturer.

166. The west side of the southern end of the Pollet looked like this before these buildings were demolished and rebuilt in 1912. The widening and modernisation of the area included the corner with Smith Street. The present-day Boot's premises and what is now Grut's shop stand in the centre background.

167. When this photograph was taken *c.*1899 Millbrook brickworks at Guelles Road, St Peter Port were operated by B. Gabriel. The works had an aqueduct and its own tramway. Land surrounding the works was farmed by William Head, whose cows are grazing in a field near the kilns. The object on the right is a large stack of hay. The photograph was taken by Aline Head.

168. The tunnel leading from Creux Harbour to Harbour Hill, Sark, looked like this before Chief Pleas decided to have it lined with concrete in 1931. Leaning against the rock face is a wooden slatted net carrier. At the far end of the tunnel is a lime kiln.

169. Mont Crevelt and South Side, St Sampson's, was uncluttered by any industrial buildings when this photograph was taken at the turn of the century. It shows a ship named *Daring*, and another with a figurehead, lying alongside west of Abraham's Bosom, where scores of small boats are now usually laid up for the winter. Photograph by Aline Head.

Sport

170. The Pelican football team were runners-up in the Jackson Cup, 1905-6. This is a photograph of the 1906 team. *From left to right, back row:* W. Golding, G. Solway, B. Denbany, S. Solway, J. Ozard, A. West, H. Trouteaud. *Middle row:* F. Jeffreys, G. White, D. Tolcher, D. Martel, P. Le Feuvre (sub-captain). *Front row:* C. Bisson, G. H. Budge (captain), A. West. Photograph by A. Laurens.

171. The Guernsey Artisans' football club, 1908-9. *From left to right, back row*: A. S. Knight (hon. treasurer), A. J. Van den Bergh (hon. secretary), N. Lihou, R. West, J. Sanson, Wm. Middlevick (president), T. Rogers and A. West (vice-presidents). *Middle row*: E. Marsh, L. Maunder, C. Baker (captain), F. Nicolle, W. Froome. *Front row*: W. Sealley, W. Elliott (sub-captain), D. Martel.

172. The Guernsey Rotary Club organised many camps in the island for poor children. In 1935 this one took place at Fort Houmet, when children from Stepney and Guernsey got together under the supervision of F. E. Fulford, the popular headmaster of the States Intermediate School for Boys.

173. The States Intermediate School cricket team in 1935. *From left to right, back row*: W. Elliott, J. Dorey, B. Bell, L. Collins, ? Duquemin. *Middle row*: ? Nunnerly, R. C. Mace, F. J. Naftel, W. C. Watling. *Front row*: J. Hartland, H. F. Nicolle, E. J. Hillier.

174. In April 1937, the Guernsey Junior Island soccer team lost 2-1 to Jersey. *From left to right, back row*: A. Le Moignan, A. Lawrence, H. Roberts, W. Coleman, M. Bridle, L. Frampton, T. Pearson, Brother Donation, A. Foster. *Middle row*: N. Le Huray, W. Martel, H. Nicolle, H. Falla, R. Robilliard, H. Le Poidevin. *Front row*: R. Brown, J. Rihoy, E. Chick, W. Falla, L. Collenette.

175. The Guernsey Hockey club team which played Jersey in March 1939 and won 2-1 at the Fort Field. *From left to right, back row*: E. Fisher, Tom Corbin, H. Nicolle, A. Cohen, R. G. Fletcher, O. Jones, P. Robilliard. *Middle row*: P. Martel, C. Palmer. R. G. Davies. *Front row*: G. Fisher, G. Ingram, F. S. Roussel.

176. In February 1938, this Elizabeth College hockey team won 4-1 against Victoria College, Jersey. *From left to right, back row*: H. T. Bichard, P. V. Carey, H. F. Nicolle, G. J. B. Green, J. M. Symes. *Middle row*: E. J. Hillier, R. C. Mace, R. H. Gwyn-Williams. *Front row*: P. de L. Le Cheminant, H. W. Bisson, R. L. S. Bichard.

177. In July 1939, the Guernsey Swimming club competed at La Vallette against the Royal Naval College, Dartmouth, watched by hundreds of spectators.

178. The Elizabeth College athletics team which beat Victoria College, Jersey 50-13 in 1938. *From left to right, back row*: R. L. S. Bichard, B. W. Rose, L. C. McKane, R. V. Burnell, J. M. Symes, H. F. Nicolle, G. J. B. Green. *Front row*: W. C. Watling, R. C. Mace, V. M. Baker.